Languages of the World

Arabic

Daniel Nunn

Heinemann
LIBRARY
Chicago, Illinois

www.capstonepub.com
Visit our website to find out more information about Heinemann-Raintree books.

To order:
☎ Phone 888-454-2279
▨ Visit www.capstonepub.com to browse our catalog and order online.

Edited by Dan Nunn and Diyan Leake
Designed by Marcus Bell
Original illustrations © Capstone Global Library Ltd 2012
Picture research by Elizabeth Alexander

Originated by Capstone Global Library Ltd
Printed and bound in China by South China Printing
  Company Ltd

15 14 13 12 11
10 9 8 7 6 5 4 3 2 1

Library of Congress Cataloging-in-Publication Data
Nunn, Daniel.
  Arabic / Daniel Nunn.—1st ed.
    p. cm.—(Languages of the world)
  Text in English and Arabic.
  Includes bibliographical references and index.
  ISBN 978-1-4329-5834-3—ISBN 978-1-4329-5842-8 (pbk.)
1. Arabic language—Textbooks for foreign speakers—English.
2. Arabic language—Grammar. 3. Arabic language—Spoken
Arabic. I. Title.
  PJ6307.N86 2012
  492.782'421—dc23   2011017914

Acknowledgments
The author and publisher are grateful to the following for permission to reproduce copyright material: Alamy pp. 10 (© Gallo Images), 16 (© Image Source), 24 (© John Warburton-Lee Photography); Corbis p. 28 (© Joshua Dalsimer); Dreamstime.com p. 27 (© Vincent Giordano); Getty Images pp. 17 (Alberto Coto/The Image Bank), 23 (Reza/Webistan); iStockphoto p. 14 (© Joel Carillet); Photolibrary pp. 5 (Ron Giling), 6 (Bruno Barbier), 7 (Celia Peterson), 12 (Grapheast), 13 (Ron Giling), 15 (Peter Widmann), 21 (Celia Peterson), 22 (Sean Sprague), 25 (Rafael Macia), 29 (Imagesource); Shutterstock pp. 8 (© mtorrell), 9 left (© Tim UR), 9 right (© grekoff), 11 (© discpicture), 18 (© Mikael Damkier), 19 (© Seleznev Oleg), 20 (© Harald Høiland Tjøstheim), 26 (© Elzbieta Sekowska).

Cover photograph reproduced with permission of Shutterstock (© Monkey Business Images).

Every effort has been made to contact copyright holders of material reproduced in this book. Any omissions will be rectified in subsequent printings if notice is given to the publisher.

Disclaimer
All the Internet addresses (URLs) given in this book were valid at the time of going to press. However, due to the dynamic nature of the Internet, some addresses may have changed, or sites may have changed or ceased to exist since publication. While the author and publisher regret any inconvenience this may cause readers, no responsibility for any such changes can be accepted by either the author or the publisher.

Contents

Arabic Around the World 4

Spoken Arabic and Standard Arabic........................... 6

Arabic and English 8

Learning Arabic 10

Saying Hello and Goodbye...................................... 12

Talking About Yourself.. 14

Asking About Others.. 16

At Home..18

Families 20

At School 22

Sports..24

Food 26

Clothes...28

Pronunciation Guide..30

Find Out More 32

Index..32

Arabic words in this book are in italics, *like this*.
You can find out how to say them by looking in the
pronunciation guide.

Arabic Around the World

Arabic is the main language of North Africa and the Middle East. It is spoken from Morocco in the west to the countries of the Arabian Peninsula in the east.

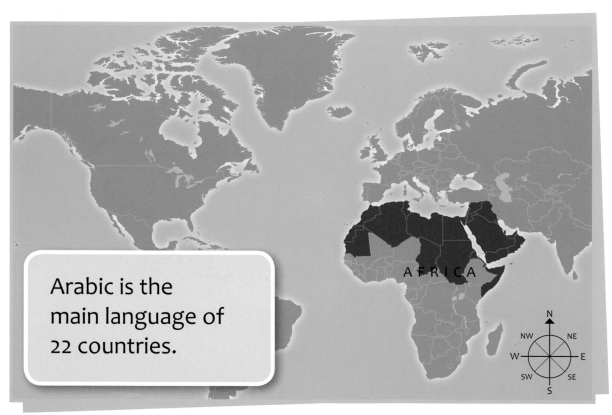

Arabic is the main language of 22 countries.

Around 80 million people in Egypt speak Arabic—more than in any other country.

Today, around 250 million people speak Arabic as their first language. Many Muslims around the world also know some Arabic. This is because Arabic is the language of the Qur'an, Islam's holy book.

Spoken Arabic and Standard Arabic

Spoken Arabic is the language spoken by ordinary people. Spoken Arabic is different from country to country. Someone from Morocco might not understand someone from Bahrain.

These Arabic speakers live in Morocco.

Arabic speakers from one country can use Standard Arabic to talk to people from other Arabic-speaking countries.

Standard Arabic is used in writing and on television and radio. Most Arabs understand it, no matter what country they are from. The Arabic in this book is Standard Arabic.

Arabic and English

Arabic is a very different language from English. It is not related to English like some other languages, such as German or French. It has its own alphabet. Some sounds in Arabic do not exist in English.

This Arabic road sign says *qif*, which means "Stop!"

The English words for fruits such as lemons, apricots, limes, and oranges all originally come from Arabic.

Even so, you may already know some Arabic words! Some of them have become part of the English language. The English words for coffee, giraffe, sugar, and jar all originally came from Arabic—*qahwa*, *zarāfa*, *sukkar*, and *jarra*.

Learning Arabic

The Arabic alphabet is very different from the alphabet used to write English. It is written from right to left. There are 28 letters in the Arabic alphabet.

This boy is learning how to write the letters of the Arabic alphabet.

This picture shows the Arabic words for "book," "writer," and "library." Can you figure out which are the letters k, t, and b?

Most words in Arabic are made from three main letters. For example, the letters k-t-b are used for words relating to writing. *Kitāb* means "book," *kātib* means "writer," and *maktaba* means "library."

Saying Hello and Goodbye

Arabs greet each other by saying, "*As-salām 'alaykum*," which means "Peace be upon you." The reply is usually "*Wa 'alaykum as-salām*," which means "And upon you, peace"!

How to say it
hello = *as-salām 'alaykum*
hello (in reply) = *wa 'alaykum as-salām*

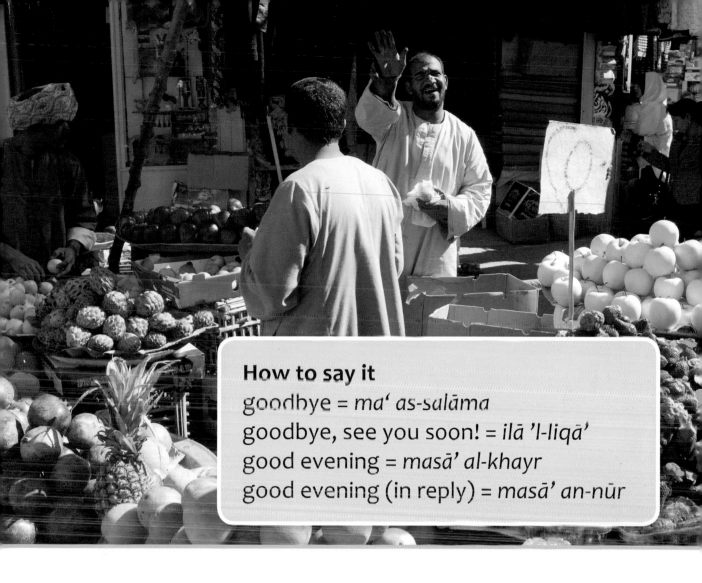

How to say it

goodbye = *ma' as-salāma*

goodbye, see you soon! = *ilā 'l-liqā'*

good evening = *masā' al-khayr*

good evening (in reply) = *masā' an-nūr*

To say goodbye, Arabs usually say, "*Ma' as-salāma.*" You can also say, "*Ilā 'l-liqā'*" if you will see the person again soon. "Good evening" is *masā' al-khayr*, to which the reply is "*Masā' an-nūr.*"

Talking About Yourself

When you meet people for the first time, they may ask what your name is. Then you can say, "*Ismī* …" and then your name.

How to say it
My name is Ali = *Ismī Ali*

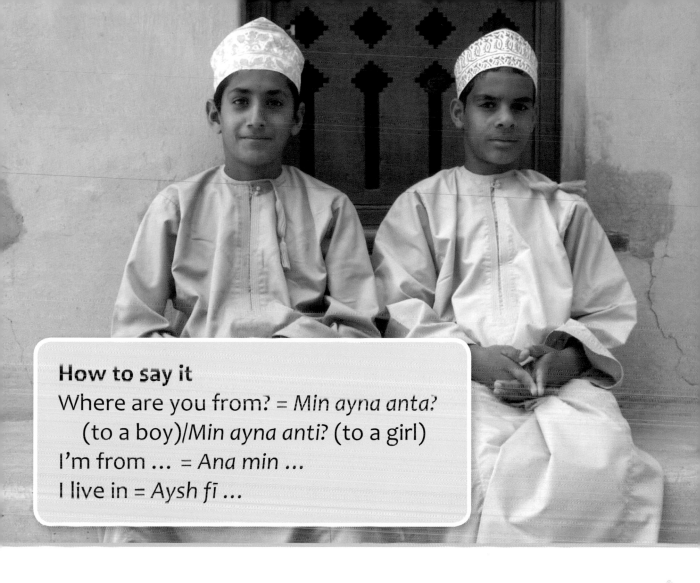

How to say it

Where are you from? = *Min ayna anta?*
    (to a boy)/*Min ayna anti?* (to a girl)
I'm from ... = *Ana min ...*
I live in = *Aysh fī ...*

Then they might ask you where you are from. You can say, "*Ana min Amreeka*" ("I am from America"). You can also say where you live: " *'Aysh fī Nyū Yūrk*" ("I live in New York").

Asking About Others

It is usually polite to ask people about themselves. The first thing people might ask is someone's name. You can say, "*Mā ismak?*" to a boy or "*Mā ismik?*" to a girl.

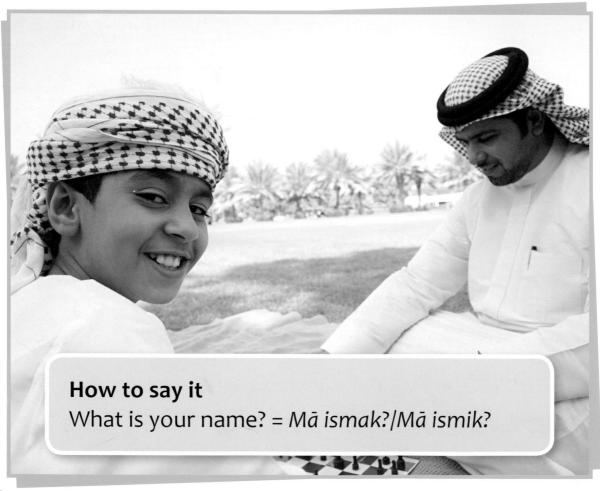

How to say it
What is your name? = *Mā ismak?/Mā ismik?*

To ask someone how they are, you say,
"*Kayf ḥālak/ḥālik?*" The answer is usually
"*Al-ḥamdu lillāh.*" This means, "Praise
be to God," but people use it to mean,
"I am well."

At Home

People's homes across the Arab world can be very different. Big cities such as Cairo and Damascus are very crowded. Most people live in apartments. Some live on the roofs of large buildings.

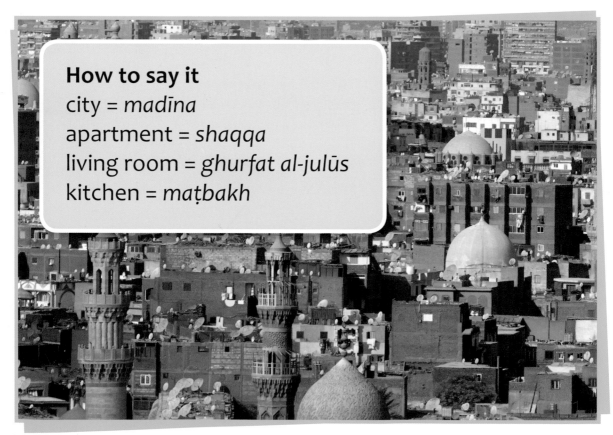

How to say it
city = *madīna*
apartment = *shaqqa*
living room = *ghurfat al-julūs*
kitchen = *maṭbakh*

In the countryside, people often live in villages. Village homes are usually small and simple. Some Bedouin Arabs live in tents. They call these *bayt al-sha'r*, which means "house of hair"!

Families

Families in many parts of the Arab world are quite large. Parents, children, aunts, uncles, cousins, and grandparents may all live close together or even share a house.

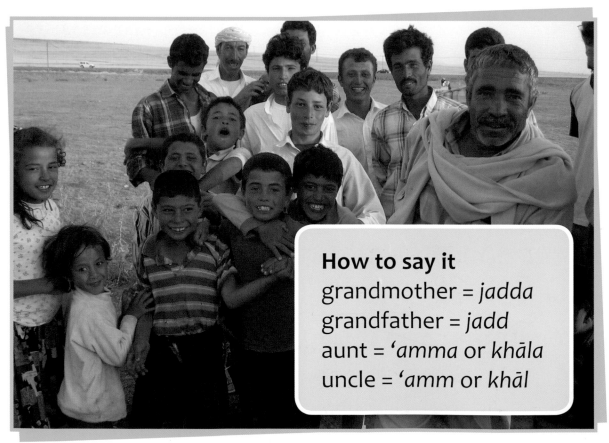

How to say it
grandmother = *jadda*
grandfather = *jadd*
aunt = *'amma* or *khāla*
uncle = *'amm* or *khāl*

How to say it
family = *usra*
father = *ab*
mother = *umm*
brother = *akh*
sister = *ukht*

Parents take on the name of their oldest son—or daughter, if they have no son. So, if they have a boy named Mazen, they are known as *Abū Mazen* ("Mazen's Father") and *Umm Mazen* ("Mazen's Mother").

At School

In most Arab countries, children go to school from Sunday to Thursday. In elementary school, boys and girls study together. When they get older, they go to separate boys' and girls' schools.

How to say it
school = *madrasa*
student = *tilmīdh* (boy)/*tilmīdha* (girl)

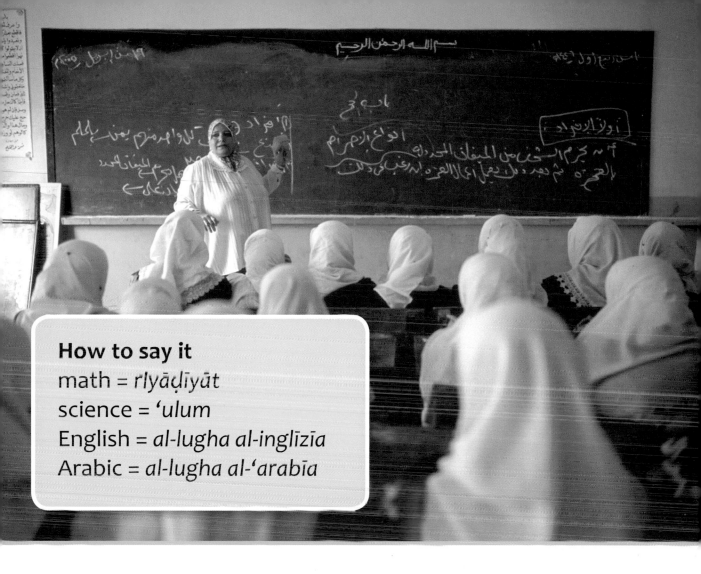

How to say it
math = *rIyāḍiyāt*
science = *'ulum*
English = *al-lugha al-inglīzīa*
Arabic = *al-lugha al-'arabīa*

Arab children learn lots of subjects at school—just like you! They study math, science, geography, history, English or French, art, and music. They also learn how to read and write Standard Arabic.

23

Sports

Soccer is very popular in most Arab countries. In Egypt the two biggest teams are Ahly and Zamalek. Other popular sports are basketball, squash, and tennis.

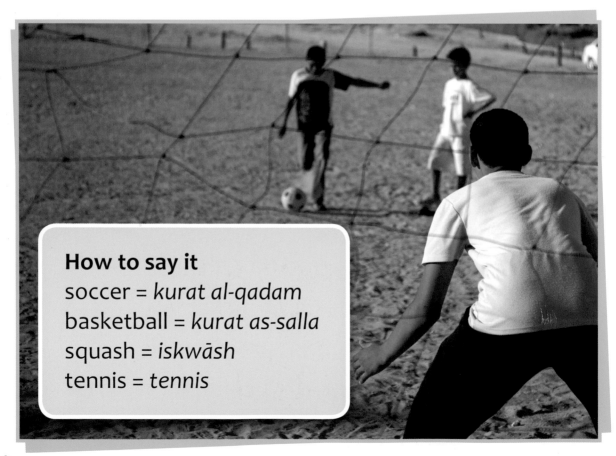

How to say it
soccer = *kurat al-qadam*
basketball = *kurat as-salla*
squash = *iskwāsh*
tennis = *tennis*

robot

How to say it
sports = *riyāḍa*
camel = *jamal*

Camel racing is a popular sport in countries such as the United Arab Emirates and Qatar. In some races, the camels are even ridden by robots instead of people!

Food

Lamb and chicken dishes served with rice are popular across the Arab world. One famous dish from Morocco is the tagine, a meaty stew cooked in a special pot.

How to say it
food = *ṭaʿām*
lamb = *laham al-kharūf*
chicken = *laham al-dajāj*
rice = *aruzz*

falafel

The most famous Arab food is from
Lebanon. There are Lebanese restaurants
all over the world. Popular Lebanese food
includes bread dipped in hummus, falafel,
and pastries filled with chopped nuts.

Clothes

In countries such as Egypt, some people wear Western-style clothing and some people wear traditional Arab clothes. Many women wear headscarves called *ḥijab*, but some women do not.

How to say it
T-shirt = *tī shirt*
pants = *banṭalūn*
shirt = *qamīṣ*
skirt = *tannūra*

This man and the boys are wearing a *dishdash*. The woman is wearing an *abaya*. These clothes are the national dress of the United Arab Emirates.

In countries such as the United Arab Emirates and Saudi Arabia, most people wear traditional Arab clothes. Men wear a long white robe called a *dishdash*. Women wear a long cloak called an *abaya*.

Pronunciation Guide

English	Arabic	Pronunciation
apartment	*shaqqa*	**shaq**-qa
Arabic	*al-lugha al-'arabīa*	al-**lu**-rra al-ara-**bee**-a
aunt	*'amma or khāla*	**am**-ma / **khaa**-la
basketball	*kurat as-salla*	**ku**-rat as-**sal**-la
Bedouin tent	*bayt al-sha'r*	**bayt** ash-**sha**-ar
book	*kitāb*	ki-**taab**
bread	*khubz*	**khubz**
brother	*akh*	**akh**
camel	*jamal*	**ja**-mal
chicken	*laham al-dajāj*	**la**-ham ad-da-**daaj**
city	*madīna*	ma-**dee**-na
English	*al-lugha al-inglīzīa*	al-**lu**-rra al-ing-lee-**zee**-a
family	*usra*	**us**-ra
father	*ab*	**ab**
food	*ṭa'ām*	ta-**aam**
giraffe	*zarāfa*	za-**raa**-fa
good evening	*masā' al-khayr*	ma-**saa** al-**khayr**
good evening (in reply)	*masā' an-nūr*	ma-**saa** an-**noor**
goodbye	*ma' as-salāma*	**ma**-a as-sa-**laa**-ma
goodbye, see you soon	*ilā l-liqā'*	i-**laa** li-**qaa**-a
grandfather	*jadd*	**jadd**
grandmother	*jadda*	**jad**-da
hello	*as-salām 'alaykum*	as-sa-**laam** a-**lay**-kum
hello (in reply)	*wa 'alaykum as-salām*	wa a-**lay**-kum as-sa-**laam**
house	*bayt*	**bayt**
How are you?	*Kayf ḥālak?* (to a boy)	**kayf haa**-lak
	Kayf ḥālik? (to a girl)	**kayf haa**-lik
I am well	*Al-ḥamdu lillāh*	al-**ham**-dul lil-**laa**

I live in …	*Aysh fī …*	**aysh fee**
I'm from …	*Ana min …*	**a**-na **min**
jar	*jarra*	**jar**-ra
kitchen	*maṭbakh*	**mat**-bakh
lamb	*laham al-kharūf*	**la**-ham al-kha-**roof**
library	*maktaba*	**mak**-ta-ba
living room	*ghurfat al-julūs*	**rrur**-fat al-ju-**loos**
math	*riyāḍīyāt*	ri-yaa-dee-**yaat**
mother	*umm*	**umm**
My name is …	*Ismī …*	is-**mee**
pants	*banṭalūn*	ban-ta-**loon**
rice	*aruzz*	a-**ruz**
salad	*salaṭa*	**sa**-la-ta
school	*madrasa*	**mad**-ra-sa
science	*'ulum*	**u**-lum
shirt	*qamīṣ*	qa-**mees**
sister	*ukht*	**ukht**
skirt	*tannura*	tan-**noo**-ra
soccer	*kurat al-qadam*	**ku**-rat al-**qa**-dam
sports	*riyāḍa*	ri-**yaa**-da
squash	*iskwāsh*	is-**kwaash**
student	*tilmīdh* (boy)/*tilmīdha* (girl)	til-**meeth** / til-**mee**-tha
sugar	*sukkar*	**suk**-kar
T-shirt	*tī shirt*	**tee**-shirt
tennis	*tennis*	**ten**-nis
tomato	*tumāta*	tu-**maa**-ta
uncle	*'amm* or *khāl*	**amm** or **khaal**
village	*qarya*	qa-**ree**-ya
What is your name?	*Mā ismak?* (to a boy)	**maa** is-mak
	Mā ismik? (to a girl)	**maa** is-mik
Where are you from?	*Min ayna anta?* (to a boy)	min **ay**-na **an**-ta
	Min ayna anti? (to a girl)	min **ay**-na **an**-ti
writer	*kātib*	**kaa**-tib

Find Out More

Books

Kudela, Katy R. *My First Book of Arabic Words* (A+ Books). North Mankato, Minn.: Capstone, 2011.

Roop, Peter, and Connie Roop. *A Visit to Egypt* (Heinemann First Library). Chicago: Heinemann Library, 2008.

Website

Learn all about the Arabic alphabet at www.funwitharabic.com.

Index

Arabian Peninsula 4
Bahrain 6
Bedouin Arabs 19
Egypt 5, 16 (Cairo), 24, 28
Lebanon 27
Morocco 4, 6, 8
Qatar 25
Saudi Arabia 29
Syria 18 (Damascus)
United Arab Emirates 25, 29